Medieval Britain

Peter Hepplewhite
with Mairi Campbell

FRANKLIN WATTS
LONDON • SYDNEY

First published in 2006 by
Franklin Watts
338 Euston Road
London NW1 3BH

Franklin Watts Australia
Hachette Children's Books
Level 17/207 Kent Street
Sydney NSW 2000

ISBN-10: 0 7496 6473 8
ISBN-13: 978 0 7496 6473 2
Dewey Classification: 720.9

Planning and production by
Discovery Books Limited
Editor: Helen Dwyer
Design: Simon Borrough
Picture Research: Rachel Tisdale

A CIP catalogue record for this book is available
from the British Library.

Printed in China

Photo credits:
Front cover top left Company of Merchant Adventurers of the City of York, top right Discovery Picture Library/Robert Humphrey, bottom left Discovery Picture Library/Paul Humphrey, bottom right Discovery Picture Library/Robert Humphrey, title page Discovery Picture Library/Robert Humphrey, 4 Discovery Picture Library/Gillian Humphrey, 5 top www.visitorkney.com, 5 right Orkney Islands Council, 5 bottom Discovery Picture Library/Paul Humphrey, 6 top Discovery Picture Library/ Robert Humphrey, 6 bottom Discovery Picture Library/Robert Humphrey, 7 top National Trust Picture Library/Ian Shaw, 7 bottom Visit Cornwall, 8 top Weald & Downland Museum, 8 bottom Peter Hepplewhite, 9 top English Heritage/Peter Dunn, 9 bottom Weald and Downland Museum, 10 Discovery Picture Library/Robert Humphrey, 11 left National Trust Picture Library/Andrew Butler, 11 right National Trust Picture Library/Nick Meers, 12 top Discovery Picture Library/Robert Humphrey, 12 bottom & 13 top Peter Hepplewhite, 13 bottom Discovery Picture Library/Gillian Humphrey, 14 top CADW, 14 bottom City of Lincoln Council, 15 top National Trust Picture Library/Matthew Antrobus, 15 bottom Roger Howard/www.photographersdirect.com, 16 top Company of Merchant Adventurers of the City of York, 16 bottom Borough Council of King's Lynn & West Norfolk, 17 top Company of Merchant Adventurers of the City of York, 17 bottom Discovery Picture Library/Robert Humphrey, 18 top Clink Prison Museum, 18 bottom Discovery Picture Library/Rachel Tisdale, 19 top Winchester Tourism, 19 bottom Nigel Morgan/West Oxfordshire District Council, 20 Discovery Picture Library/Gillian Humphrey, 21 top Discovery Picture Library/Robert Humphrey, 21 bottom Chris Graham/www.photographersdirect.com, 22 top & bottom Discovery Picture Library/Robert Humphrey, 23 top Peter Hepplewhite, 23 bottom Roger Howard/ www.photographersdirect.com, 24 top CADW, 24 bottom CADW, 25 top Discovery Picture Library/Alex Ramsay, 25 bottom Peter Hepplewhite, 26 top Roger Howard, 26 bottom & 27 top Peter Hepplewhite, 27 bottom CADW, 28 Peter Hepplewhite, 29 left CADW, 29 right Historic Royal Palaces

CONTENTS

AN AGE OF CONTRASTS

Have you ever stood behind the battlements of a castle or climbed a cathedral tower? They are spectacular buildings that have lasted from medieval times (also called the Middle Ages). This fascinating age began in 1066, when the Normans, a people from northern France, invaded England. It ended when Henry VII took the throne for the Tudor family in 1485.

Built in stone

The medieval buildings that we see today still make a great impact on the landscape. They were built in long-lasting stone and even in ruins they tell us what was important to people in those distant times.

Castles were built to protect and control the countryside. Ludlow Castle in Shropshire is one of a series of fortresses built along the border between England and Wales. At that time, the border was one of the most dangerous places in medieval Britain.

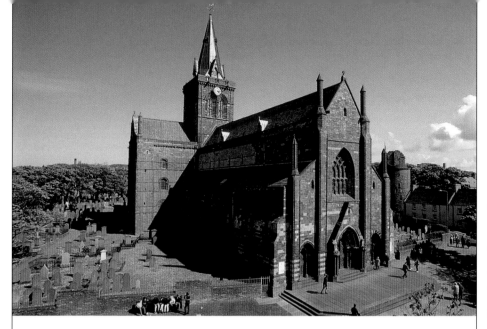

St Magnus Cathedral, Orkney. This 12th-century cathedral was built in the Romanesque style popular at the time, with rounded arches above windows and doors.

Mighty castles stamped the power of great lords across the country, while soaring cathedrals were built to show the glory of God. These memorable places also reveal the great skills of the architects, masons and carpenters of the time.

Rebuilding the past

The buildings of ordinary people have not survived so well. Even though countless peasants' huts were built, few are left today. They were constructed from materials that have not lasted, such as wood and mud. The work of archaeologists tells us what these huts were like and has helped museums build reconstructions. Visiting these 'new' medieval buildings brings the past to life for modern visitors.

This 14th-century manor house (background) at Lower Brockhampton in Herefordshire is cared for by the National Trust. It is surrounded by a narrow moat that you can cross through a crooked gatehouse (at the front).

MASONS' MARKS

In the Middle Ages there were few drawings for buildings. The ideas of the architect, or person in charge, were brought to reality by a master mason. Masons travelled round in teams and their stone-carving skills were passed on from father to son. They carved symbols and patterns in the stone, like these at St Magnus Cathedral in the Orkney Islands, Scotland, to show who had done the carving. Masons registered their marks with masons' guilds so no one else could use them.

THE MANOR HOUSE

In medieval times most people were peasants living in small villages. The lord of the manor was the most important person in their lives. He allowed the peasants to farm some of his land to grow food for their families. In return they had to pay him dues, or taxes. This meant working for him several days a week and giving him some of the goods they produced on their farms. This system was called the feudal system.

Life in a manor house

The lord of the manor lived in the best home in the village, the manor house. Some manor houses, like Stokesay Castle in Shropshire (above and below), were built of stone and often had defences such as a moat or battlements to protect them from attackers.

The great hall was the centre of manor life, where the lord entertained guests or judged criminals. Servants and soldiers slept crowded together on straw in the great hall. The lord and his family had their own bedroom, which was known as the solar. As in Stokesay, this was usually on the first floor, next to the hall.

Stokesay Castle is really a fortified manor house, even though it is called a castle. It was built around 1281-91 by a wealthy wool merchant, Lawrence of Ludlow. Lawrence needed a licence from the king to build the battlements (the area along the top of walls where soldiers could stand and fire at attackers). You can see the battlements in the background of this photograph.

The great hall at Stokesay is almost unchanged since medieval times. The large gabled windows (with tops shaped like a triangle) were designed to let in lots of light. Can you see the window seats and the supports for the wooden roof beams?

Most manor houses were abandoned or rebuilt over the centuries so there are few left in original condition today. Sometimes you have to be a building detective and pick out the medieval architecture from changes made in later times.

The Old Post Office at Tintagel in Cornwall was built in the 14th century as a home for an independent farmer (see page 9). One room was used as a post office in Victorian times. Today the building is in the care of the National Trust.

RESTORING IGHTHAM MOTE

Caring for medieval buildings is very expensive. Over the last 15 years the National Trust – the biggest owner of historic buildings in Britain – has spent £10,000,000 restoring Ightham Mote, a fortified manor house near Sevenoaks in Kent (below). The building was completely taken apart and rebuilt. In the picture the masonry is being restored. During the restoration, the Trust builders kept finding shoes that had been hidden by past owners to ward off evil spirits.

SEE FOR YOURSELF

You can visit some fine manor houses across Britain. Here are some well-known examples:
1 Spofforth Castle, North Yorkshire
2 Stokesay Castle, Shropshire
3 Lower Brockhampton, Worcestershire
4 Ightham Mote, Kent
5 Hever Castle, Kent
6 Penshurst Place, Kent

A Peasant's Home

Most communities during the Middle Ages were little more than hamlets – places that have no more than 10–50 homes. Peasants were very poor as they had to pay much of their income to their lord. A peasant's home was therefore very simple.

A typical home was built with a wooden frame. The spaces in the frame were filled with wattle and daub. Wattle was a framework of twigs. Daub was a mixture of mud, straw and manure that dried in the sun to give a strong building material.

A reconstruction of a 13th-century cottage made of flint at the Weald and Downland Museum in West Sussex. The cottage is based on the remains of two cottages excavated by archaeologists at Hangleton near Brighton.

Roofs and chimneys

Food was cooked on an open hearth so there were no chimneys. The roofs were thatched with straw or reeds and the floors made from hard-packed earth or clay.

Some medieval homes did not have chimneys, but sometimes they had smoke holes in the roof like the flint and thatch cottage at the Weald and Downland Museum.

Deserted medieval villages

Some of the best information about peasant cottages has come from the work of archaeologists in deserted medieval villages. There are a thousand of these ghostly communities across Britain, more than 200 in the county of Norfolk alone. Usually all that you can see of deserted medieval villages today are low mounds and ditches that show the outlines of settlements.

An artist's impression of Wharram Percy, a deserted medieval village. You can still see the foundations of more than 30 medieval peasant houses at this site near Malton in North Yorkshire.

Once historians thought there was one terrible reason for most of these abandoned settlements – the Black Death. This killer disease wiped out more than a third of the population in the mid-14th century. But today a less dramatic cause is blamed for many deserted medieval villages – sheep. Wool became big business in medieval times. Lords turned many fields into pasture for sheep and forced the peasants to leave.

Independent farmers

Later in the Middle Ages, when the feudal system was not so strict, some hard-working peasants were able to buy their own land and became independent farmers. The wealthiest were able to build quite grand homes that looked like small manor houses.

This rather grand late medieval house has been reconstructed at the Weald and Downland Museum in West Sussex. You can see the wooden posts holding it up. The walls between the timbers are filled in with wattle and daub.

TAXES FOR THE CHURCH

As well as the taxes they had to pay to their lords, peasants paid another tax to the church, which was very rich and powerful and played a large part in everyone's lives. This tax was called a tithe and was about one-tenth of all the peasants' produce.

Payment or punishment

The tithe could be paid in money but more often it was paid in goods such as crops or seeds. It may not seem a lot to us but it could mean a family went hungry or had no seeds left to plant next year's crop. If families did not pay, the church could arrest and punish them.

Tithe barns

Often the tithe brought in so many crops that powerful churchmen built great barns to store them. These were called tithe barns. A few huge tithe barns survive to tell us more about the hard lives of ordinary medieval people. Leigh Court Barn in Worcestershire (below) is one of the largest surviving medieval barns.

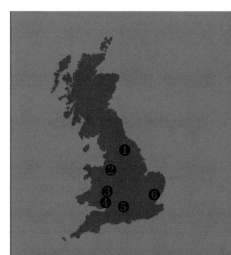

SEE FOR YOURSELF
A few barns and mills still survive from medieval times.
1 Fountains Abbey Watermill, Yorkshire
2 Nether Alderley Mill, Cheshire
3 Leigh Court Barn, Worcestershire
4 Ashleworth Tithe Barn, Gloucestershire
5 Great Coxwell Barn, Oxfordshire
6 Priors Hall Barn, Essex

This tithe barn, Leigh Court Barn, was built in the 14th century for the monks of Pershore Abbey. It has pairs of curved timbers holding it up, called a cruck frame.

Some tithe barns had immense cruck frames and steeply sloping tiled roofs. Others like Great Coxwell Barn in Oxfordshire (below and right) were made of local stone. The food stored in the barns was sold at local markets or kept for times when the harvest was poor.

Great Coxwell Barn is so big that tall aisle posts (above) were needed to help support the high roof.

Great Coxwell Barn is made of Cotswold stone and roofed with slate tiles. There are several slit windows, two porches and one pair of doors. Can you see the small, square holes in the walls? These are called putlocks and were the places where the scaffolding poles rested while the barn was being built.

Mills

Life must have seemed an endless round of taxes. Every manor had a mill to grind corn, but it belonged to the lord. Since it was against the law for peasants to grind their own corn, they had to pay to use their lord's mill. You can visit and walk around a 15th-century corn mill at Nether Alderley in Cheshire.

Mills were built for other uses as well as to grind corn. In fulling mills wool was cleaned to make cloth. A water channel brought a stream to the mill to work a water wheel. This drove hammers that pounded the cloth in big stone vats.

CELEBRATION AND WORSHIP

Almost every town and village in Britain has at least one medieval church, reflecting the importance of faith in the Middle Ages. The church was the focus of community life and everyone gathered in their local church on Sundays and Holy Days.

Holy Days

Sundays and Holy Days were the only days ordinary people did not work. At Christmas, Easter and on saints' days there would be feasting, drinking and dancing. The church porch would hold stalls during fairs and festivals. Sometimes porches, like Kilpeck Church in Herefordshire (right), were decorated with stone carvings from scenes in the Bible or local events.

Church styles and structures

The earliest medieval churches were built in the Norman style. They were constructed of stone with plain, rounded arches, heavy pillars and small windows. Later churches were built in the new Gothic style with high ceilings and large pointed windows.

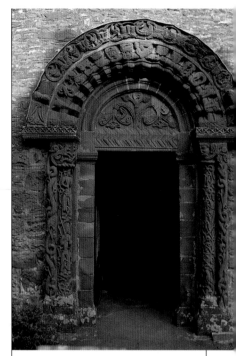

Kilpeck Church doorway has some unique sandstone carvings, including soldiers and angels. The carvings are in a similar style to those on the font on the opposite page.

St Mary's Church at Lastingham in North Yorkshire. St Mary's is a Norman church with a 15th-century bell tower. The crypt was built as a shrine to St Cedd, an Anglo-Saxon bishop. Pilgrims came from all over Britain to pray here.

St Peter and St Paul's Church in Pickering, North Yorkshire. Wall paintings like these were not just for decoration. They were also a way of teaching people important Christian stories at a time when few could read. This one shows the death of Saint Edmund, an English king murdered by the Vikings.

Churches were usually divided into three parts: the chancel where the priest conducted the service, the bell tower and the nave where the villagers stood. In a typical village church there were no seats. When sermons became longer, benches were provided. The walls were decorated with carvings and vivid paintings.

The square-shaped chancel held the altar, the most important feature of the church where the priest celebrated Mass (the Catholic service). Nearby would be the piscina, a small sink for washing the ceremonial vessels after the service. Most village churches had floors of beaten earth or cobbles but building materials varied across the country. In some Yorkshire churches, for example, slabs of local stone were used for flooring.

Most people today do not go to church every Sunday. However, many families do go to church to have their babies christened or baptised. This ceremony welcomes the baby into the Christian faith. During the service the baby is sprinkled with holy water from a font. The beautifully carved early medieval font pictured below is in Eardisley Church, Herefordshire.

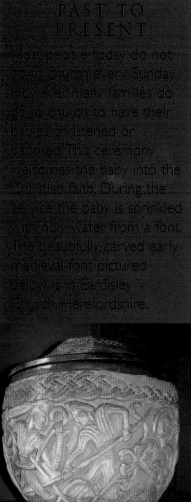

TOWN LIFE

In medieval times most towns were small, noisy and very smelly. Sometimes the streets had cobbles, but often they were unsurfaced and had open drains running along them. Important towns were surrounded by high walls for protection. The gates were closed at night and opened again at daybreak.

This aerial photograph shows Conwy castle and the impressive walls protecting the town. They were built on the orders of King Edward I after his conquest of north Wales in 1282.

Town houses

Land inside the walls was expensive so town houses were tall and narrow. They were built with wood uprights to support the roof. The walls were filled in with wattle and daub. In the 13th century clay or stone roof tiles became popular because they were less likely to catch fire than thatch (straw or reed).

The Jew's House in Lincoln dates back to the 12th century and is one of the oldest houses in Britain. The ornate entrance arch shows it was built for a wealthy family. In the Middle Ages Lincoln had a flourishing Jewish community with traders, moneylenders and merchants.

This is Aberconwy House in Conwy, Wales, built in the late 14th century. You can see the top floor is supported by two lower stone-built floors and that it hangs out over the street.

Inside town houses

Houses belonging to wealthy merchants had several floors, and glass windows instead of wooden shutters – a real luxury that let in light and kept out the cold. The ground floor was a large hall with a central hearth. Upstairs were the family rooms, sitting room and bedrooms. The upper floors projected out over the street so that the rooms were as big as possible. Open fires were used for cooking and the kitchens were separate buildings in backyards to help prevent fire spreading.

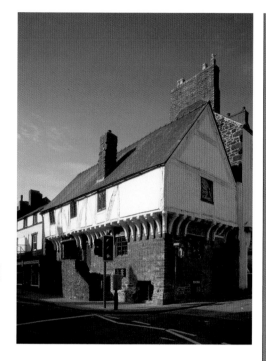

SEE FOR YOURSELF

Medieval features can still be seen in towns all over the country.
In Newcastle-upon-Tyne (1) the town walls remain today. York (2) still has medieval walls, gateways, streets and buildings. Market crosses survive in Burnley (3) and Chester (4). In Conwy (5) you can visit Aberconwy House, the castle and walk around the town walls. King's Lynn (6) still has two medieval guildhalls and a merchant's warehouse.

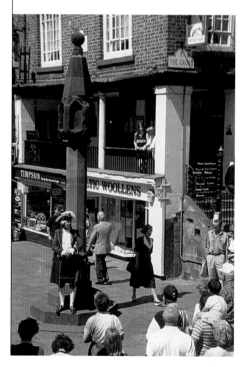

Workrooms and shops

In larger towns people who worked in the same trade often lived in the same street. Craftsmen worked from their homes and sold their goods from workrooms that opened on to the street.

This medieval sandstone cross marks the centre of the fortified town of Chester. Markets were held here once a week. Peasants laid their goods on the ground while richer traders had stalls to display their products.

STREET NAMES

We can learn more about the layout of medieval towns from surviving street names. Names like Baker Street, Brewhouse Lane, Threadneedle Street and Tanners (men who made animal skins into leather) Lane tell us what happened in these streets.

15

GUILDS AND CRAFTS

Most medieval towns had a grand guildhall. Guilds were clubs, set up for three main groups. The most powerful guilds were associations of merchants who controlled local trade. Next came guilds formed by craftsmen, such as tailors or tanners. They made rules about the quality of goods they sold and the training of apprentices. Finally there were religious guilds, people coming together to serve God, perhaps by helping the poor.

The lower part of the Merchant Adventurers' Hall in York is made from brick. These bricks were the first made in York since the Romans left almost 1,000 years before the hall was built.

Guildhalls

Guildhalls were lively and busy places used for meetings, prayers, feasts, dances and putting on plays. The Merchant Adventurers' Hall in York (above) was built between 1357 and 1361 and is one of the oldest left in Britain. The undercroft in York was used as an almshouse (home for the poor) and there are still scorch marks left by candles that stood in niches in the walls. The Trinity Guildhall in King's Lynn (below) was built in the 1420s by the Guild of the Trinity and is an indication of their wealth.

Trinity Guildhall in King's Lynn has a fine Gothic window and a spectacular chequerboard exterior consisting of squares of black flint and white stone. Today the building is part of King's Lynn town hall.

The complicated timber frame of the Merchant Adventurers' Hall in York was put together piece by piece. The carpenters marked all the timbers in their workshops and used these marks to assemble the whole frame. You can still see the marks today.

Guild buildings

Guilds designed coats of arms showing details of their work. As well as guildhalls they often built their own schools and retirement homes, and looked after old and sick guild members. The guilds also provided the townspeople with entertainment, performing colourful, religious plays in market places or churchyards.

PAST TO PRESENT

The photograph below shows the courtyard of Lord Leycester Hospital in Warwick. It was built in the late 14th century by the religious guilds of St Mary and St George. The guilds used the premises for meeting rooms and living quarters until they were taken over by Robert Dudley, Earl of Leicester, in 1571. He turned them into a 'hospital' – a home for disabled soldiers and their wives. Today, the Lord Leycester Hospital is home to eight ex-servicemen who live in modernised flats and help to look after the building. The white bear and staff you can see on the black and white building is the coat of arms of the Earl of Leicester.

CRIME AND POVERTY

Medieval buildings can tell us a great deal about the way criminals and the poor were treated. Have you heard the phrase 'you'll end up in the Clink'? It means you'll end up in prison. Clink was a famous London jail that got its name from the clinking sound of the prisoners' chains.

As in all medieval prisons, conditions in Clink were terrible. The prisoners were beaten, tortured and if they had no money to buy food they starved. Although some towns like London built special prisons, most like York or Norwich used the dungeons of the town castle. For many being sent to jail was as good as a death sentence. In 1358, 50 prisoners died in York Castle alone. Most castles have a dungeon or prison you can visit.

Stocks and pillories

For small crimes people had their legs fastened in stocks or their heads in pillories. This might not sound harsh but passers by would shout at them or throw mud and stones. Many towns and villages still have stocks you can visit in market places or churchyards.

These prisoners' chains are on display in the Clink Museum in London, which is on the site of the medieval prison.

A law passed in 1351 stated that every community had to have a set of stocks like these in the market place at Ludlow in Shropshire.

Hospitals and almshouses

Many poor people lived miserable lives, unless they were lucky enough to be cared for in hospitals or almshouses. The word hospital comes from the Latin word 'hospes' which means guest. In early medieval times monks and nuns ran hospitals like the one in Winchester (below) to look after travellers, but gradually they changed to care for the poor, the old and the sick.

The Hospital of St Cross in Winchester was founded by Henry de Blois between 1132 and 1136 to look after the poor. It is Britain's oldest charitable building and still cares for a community of elderly men, known as 'the bretheren'. In this picture you are looking at the main entrance from the courtyard.

Almshouses were similar to hospitals but they were built by rich people who believed they could get to heaven by giving charity to the poor. You can see medieval almshouses like these in Burford (pictured below) all over the country.

These splendid almshouses in Burford, Oxfordshire, were founded in 1457 by the Earl of Warwick. They are stone built with tiled roofs and have carved detailed patterns around the windows.

19

TRAVEL AND TRANSPORT

A remarkable range of evidence survives to help building detectives find out about travel and transport in medieval times. Country tracks, inns and bridges survive as evidence of once thriving trades.

Drove roads

Wool was England's greatest industry and thousands of packhorses carried wool from inland pastures to ports for export to Europe. Drovers too were a common sight, moving herds of cattle, sheep or even geese to markets, sometimes hundreds of kilometres away. Drove roads had wide grass verges, bordered by hedges where animals could graze at night. The roads were not surfaced and often turned to mud in heavy rain.

Inns

Travellers needed places to rest and eat, and many towns and villages still have pubs or hotels that date back to the Middle Ages. One famous example is the New Inn in Gloucester. This was built around 1430 to cater for pilgrims who came to pray in the cathedral. It still has a medieval courtyard with galleries on all sides.

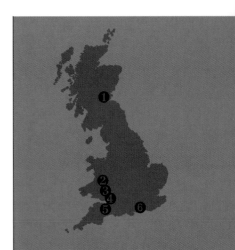

SEE FOR YOURSELF
A few medieval inns and bridges can still be seen:
1 Old Bridge, Stirling
2 Rhydspence Inn, Whitney-on-Wye, Herefordshire
3 Monnow Bridge, Monmouth
4 New Inn, Gloucester
5 The George and Pilgrims Inn, Glastonbury, Somerset
6 Stopham Bridge, West Sussex

The Rhydspence Inn near the River Wye on the borders of Herefordshire and Powys. It was built in the 14th century as a medieval manor house, but since it was on a drover's track it eventually became a stopping place for drovers.

The Monnow Bridge in Monmouth was built in the 14th century and still has a defensive gate and portcullis. However, the River Monnow is quite shallow here and this gate was probably only built to look impressive.

Bridges

Bridges were vital links in the road network and the most important feature of many riverside settlements. In some walled towns something unusual happened to their bridges – there was such a shortage of building land that houses and shops were built on them. Unfortunately none of these bridges survives today. The most famous British example was London Bridge built in the 12th century. This lasted for more than 600 years before it was replaced in 1831.

Stirling Old Bridge in Scotland was built at the end of the Middle Ages. Customs men sat in a covered booth in the middle of the bridge and charged taxes on goods entering the town.

CATHEDRALS

The finest buildings of the medieval period, the cathedrals, still attract millions of visitors every year. These great churches were headquarters for the bishops – priests who oversee a region. The architects who designed them were attempting to create buildings that glorified God and impressed ordinary people with His power. It took hundreds of skilled craftsmen decades of work to turn the architects' grand schemes into reality.

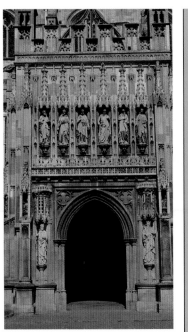

The front of Gloucester Cathedral was built and carved in the 13th century. The carvings of human figures are more lifelike than those of slightly earlier medieval buildings.

Cathedral plans

When you look at cathedrals from above you can see they were built in the shape of a cross. The east end had the altar and bishop's throne. The west end was a huge nave (hall) where the people stood or knelt. An elaborate stone screen divided the people from the priests and monks. Outside were the cloisters. These were elegant covered walkways that linked different buildings.

SEE FOR YOURSELF

There are many impressive cathedrals in Britain that you can visit. Here are a few:
1 St Magnus Cathedral, Orkney
2 Dunblane Cathedral, Stirling
3 Glasgow Cathedral
4 Durham Cathedral
5 York Minster
6 Lincoln Cathedral
7 St David's Cathedral, Pembrokeshire
8 Gloucester Cathedral
9 Wells Cathedral
10 Salisbury Cathedral
11 Winchester Cathedral
12 Exeter Cathedral

This picture shows the intricate ceiling of the cloisters at Gloucester Cathedral. The pattern is called fan vaulting because of its shape. The vaulting holds up the roof but looks impressive too.

Cathedral styles

The earliest cathedrals were built in the Romanesque style. This means they had round arches above the windows and doors, and massive rounded columns. Thick walls were needed to support the roof. Durham and Wells cathedrals show some of these features.

Later cathedrals were built in the more airy Gothic style. Architects had discovered how to build roofs resting on rows of pillars instead of on solid walls. Now they could have larger stained-glass windows that let in lots of light. The weight of the roof was supported by projecting buttresses – elegant, arched, stone or brick supports on the outside of the building.

SEEKING SANCTUARY

A person in trouble with the law could seek refuge or sanctuary at a cathedral or church. At Durham they were safe once they had grasped hold of the knocker pictured here. If the person confessed to his crime and gave up his weapons, he was allowed to stay for 40 days. After this he had to surrender or promise to leave the country. If he chose to leave he had to walk barefoot, carrying a cross, to the nearest port.

Salisbury Cathedral in Wiltshire is a fine example of a cathedral built in the Gothic style, largely in the 13th century. You can join a tour and climb 332 steps to the base of the magnificent spire. At 123 metres high it is the tallest in England.

ABBEYS AND MONASTERIES

Cathedrals and churches are not the only reminders of medieval faith. Across the country there are the remains of hundreds of abbeys and monasteries, often in remote and beautiful sites. These religious communities were places where monks or nuns lived and worked together to devote their lives to God.

Tintern Abbey in Monmouthshire was founded in 1131 and rebuilt between 1269 and 1301. At the peak of the abbey's fame 400 monks lived there. This photograph shows the ruins of the abbey church.

Expanding monasteries

In 1066 there were only 50 monasteries but by 1320 there were 900. Some remained small and isolated, while others, like Fountains Abbey in North Yorkshire, became the centres of rich and powerful estates employing hundreds of workers.

Monastery life

Monasteries were busy places. Monks and nuns had to attend church services six times a day, starting at 2 a.m. The monastery also played an important part in the life of the local community. It was a landowner and an employer. The monks cared for the sick and offered travellers a place to stay. They also ran schools and were responsible for looking after ancient books and making copies of them.

Ewenny Priory, Vale of Glamorgan, was founded in 1141 by monks who followed the teachings of St Benedict. The roof is held up by the simple but strong barrel vaulting (curved arches) you can clearly see in this photograph.

These beautiful and spectacular ruins are all that remain of the once magnificent Fountains Abbey in North Yorkshire. This was founded in 1132 and became one of the largest abbeys in Europe.

Living quarters

While the church was at the centre of monastery life, around it were the monks' living and working quarters. The monks spent much of their time in the cloisters (covered walkways) where they strolled and studied. The cloisters also linked different parts of the building, including the dormitory where the monks slept, the dining room and the chapter house where meetings took place.

Most medieval abbeys and monasteries are now in ruins because they were taken over and sold by King Henry VIII in the 1530s. Their new owners usually tore them down to reuse their building materials, especially the lead and timber from the roofs.

SEE FOR YOURSELF

You can see the remains of medieval abbeys and monasteries across Britain:
1 Dryburgh Abbey, near Melrose, Scottish Borders
2 Jedburgh Abbey, Borders
3 Dundrennan Abbey, Dumfries and Galloway
4 Sweetheart Abbey, Dumfries and Galloway
5 Rievaulx Abbey, North Yorkshire
6 Fountains Abbey, North Yorkshire
7 Valle Crucis Abbey, Clwyd
8 Ewenny Priory, Vale of Glamorgan
9 Tintern Abbey, Monmouthshire
10 Lacock Abbey, Wiltshire
11 Michelham Priory, Sussex

THE GREEN MAN

Images of the Green Man, like this ornamental carving at Lacock Abbey, are often found in medieval buildings. You can see him carved in stone or wood, painted on stained glass, or drawn in illuminated manuscripts. The Green Man is usually shown as a startling face, with some leaves sprouting from his mouth, nose, eyes or ears. No one knows for certain what the Green Man represents, but it is likely he is meant to be a memory of an ancient god of the woods or the spirit of nature.

Castles are one of the most exciting features of our medieval heritage. A castle was a fortress built by a noble, but it was also a home for his family, the place from which he ran his estates and a symbol of his wealth and power.

Norman power bases

The first castles were built when Britain was a dangerous place to live, with frequent wars and rebellions. Many castles go back to the years after 1066 when Norman barons erected castles to control their new lands. Some of these Norman families were extremely powerful. The de Warennes family, for example, built castles at Conisborough in South Yorkshire, Castle Acre in Norfolk and Sandal in West Yorkshire.

Motte and bailey

The earliest castles were built of wood, often on an artificial mound of earth or broken rock called a motte. Usually the motte was protected by a bailey (a walled courtyard).

PAST TO PRESENT

Many castles have appeared in films. Bamburgh, a 12th-century fortress in Northumberland (above), stands on a huge rock next to the sea. This dramatic setting earned the castle a role as Maid Marian's family home in *Robin Hood, Prince of Thieves* (1991). Nearby Alnwick Castle was built by the powerful Percy family in the 12th century. Still the home of the Duke of Northumberland, Alnwick was used as Hogwarts school for wizards in *Harry Potter and the Philosopher's Stone* (2001).

This view shows the motte, with the stone keep on top, at Pickering Castle in North Yorkshire. Imagine how hard it would be for an attacker to climb this steep hill.

Stone castles

By the 12th century many castles had been rebuilt in stone with huge towers called keeps like the one pictured right. They had walls up to 10 metres thick to protect them from attack by catapults

Orford Castle in Suffolk (left) was started by King Henry II in 1265. This has a polygonal (many-sided) keep, the only one in Britain.

or by tunnels. At the end of the 13th century during his conquest of Wales, King Edward I built a series of castles including Caernarfon, Harlech, Conwy and Beaumaris (pictured below).

Beaumaris Castle, on the Isle of Anglesey, was part of the ring of castles built by Edward I to conquer Wales. Started in 1295, Beaumaris is a concentric castle. That means it has two sets of strong walls studded with towers.

During the 14th and 15th centuries the country was more peaceful and castles were being built to impress. Rich nobles built grand castles to prove that they had been successful in life. The Scrope family built Bolton Castle in North Yorkshire with eight suites for guests.

DEADLY DETAILS

Next time you visit a castle, walk around it slowly and imagine you are leading an attack. Look out for the deadly features that would have made the castle so difficult to capture.

Battlements and arrow loops

You lead your soldiers forwards, looking anxiously at the high curtain walls and flanking towers. Suddenly archers open fire from behind the safety of battlements and arrow loops (the narrow slits in the wall). Under a hail of arrows your troops fill the encircling ditch. They use faggots (bundles of sticks) to build a bridge to the gatehouse and pack earth and stones on top to make a rough roadway. Then a battering ram is pushed forward. Many men fall injured or die on the short journey.

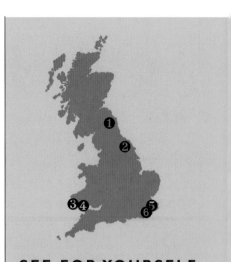

SEE FOR YOURSELF

1 Warkworth Castle, Northumberland

2 Castle Bolton, North Yorkshire
A 14th-century castle that had a portcullis on every external door.

3 Manorbier Castle, Pembrokeshire
You can see the chamber for the drawbridge winding gear.

4 Kidwelly Castle, Carmarthenshire
Find the murder holes on the main gate.

5 Rochester Castle, Kent

6 Pevensey Castle, East Sussex
Look out for the fine curtain walls and round towers.

Arrow loops allowed defenders to shoot from cover, while attackers found them difficult to hit. These loops in Grey Mare's Tail Tower at Warkworth Castle in Northumberland are four metres long.

Portcullises and murder holes

Finally, the drawbridge and strong wooden gates are battered down and you lead the charge forward – only to be stopped by the criss-cross shape of the portcullis. While your bravest knights hack at this with axes, the defenders pour boiling water or pitch (hot, liquid tar) through machicolations in the entrance passage (below). It is no wonder that machicolations are sometimes known as murder holes.

Castle under siege

When you finally break through to the courtyard you find it deserted. The defenders have pulled back into the mighty keep. Now you will have to starve them into surrender and if their cellars are full of supplies that could take months.

You can clearly see the machicolations at the top of this photograph of one of the gatehouses at Beaumaris Castle, Isle of Anglesey.

This photograph shows the winding mechanism for the portcullis at the Tower of London.

TIMELINE

1066 William, Duke of Normandy, invades England and becomes king after defeating King Harold II at the Battle of Hastings.

1078 King William I begins building the Tower of London.

1090 Ely and Norwich Cathedrals are begun.

1093 Durham Cathedral is begun.

1131 Tintern Abbey is founded.

1135 Fountains Abbey is founded.

1180 Wells Cathedral is begun.

1209 London Bridge is completed.

1245 The rebuilding of Westminster Abbey is begun.

1265 First parliament to include elected representatives from the towns and counties meets.

1284–1307 King Edward I takes control of Wales and builds several large castles including Beaumaris, Harlech, Conwy and Caernarfon.

1296–1314 England at war with Scotland.

1320 Scottish independence recognized by King Edward III.

1337–1453 Hundred Years' War between England and France.

1348 The Black Death reaches England, leading to the deaths of half the population.

1410 University of St Andrew's, Fife, Scotland, is founded.

1455–1471 Civil war in England known as the Wars of the Roses between the royal families of Lancaster and York.

1485 Henry Tudor defeats King Richard III at the Battle of Bosworth and becomes the first Tudor king.

GLOSSARY

abbey large monastery or convent headed by an abbot or abbess.

alms food or money given to poor people.

apprentice boy who learned his skills in the home of a master craftsman.

battering ram a large wooden beam used to break down walls and gates.

coat of arms a family's emblem.

cruck pairs of curved timbers to support an upper storey or roof.

crypt an underground chamber in a church.

curtain walls the outer walls of the castle.

drovers herders who moved animals over long distances.

estates large farms.

flanking towers towers that stick out beyond the walls, giving less cover to attackers.

Gothic style of building from 1150 to 1400 with high ceilings and large pointed windows.

guild group of craftsmen.

hamlet small settlement.

heritage a feature that survives from the past.

keep the strongest tower inside a castle.

mason someone who makes things out of stone.

monastery religious community of monks or nuns, usually smaller than an abbey.

niche a recess in a wall.

peasant poor farmer or farm labourer.

pillory a wooden frame similar to stocks with holes for head and hands.

portcullis a gate made of wood or metal, which protected the entrance to a medieval castle.

Romanesque medieval style of architecture inspired by the Romans with thick walls, round arches and small windows.

stocks a wooden frame with holes for the feet in which criminals were put for punishment.

tanner person who treated animal skins to make leather.

vaulting curved arches.

PLACES TO VISIT

Beaumaris Castle, Isle of Anglesey
www.cadw.wales.gov.uk (type Beaumaris into 'search site')
Begun in 1295, this unfinished castle is a great example of a concentrically planned castle.

Caernarfon Castle, Gwynedd
www.cadw.wales.gov.uk (type Caernarfon into 'search site')
The seat of medieval English government in Wales. It has many passageways and wall walks.

Caerphilly Castle
www.cadw.wales.gov.uk (type Caerphilly into 'search site')
One of the largest medieval fortresses in Britain.

Chester, Cheshire
www.chester.gov.uk (click tourism and leisure)
In the Middle Ages, several towers and gates were added to the Roman walls.

Conwy, Gwynedd
Conwy's medieval walls with 22 towers remain unbroken today.

Harlech Castle, Gwynedd
www.cadw.wales.gov.uk (type Harlech into 'search site')
Looking seawards, Harlech's late 13th-century battlements are on a near vertical cliff face.

King's Lynn, Norfolk
One of the leading seaports in England in the medieval period. Medieval buildings include the Hanseatic warehouse and the Trinity Guildhall.

Museum of London
www.museumoflondon.org.uk/english
The Medieval London gallery explores the city's history from Saxon to Tudor times.

Norwich, Norfolk
Norwich's 33 medieval churches were built with the profits of the wool trade. The cathedral has the largest monastic cloisters in England. Its white stone was quarried in Normandy, France.

Salisbury Cathedral, Wiltshire
www.salisburycathedral.org.uk
The Cathedral was begun in 1220. The spire was built in 1320 and is the tallest church spire in the UK at 123 metres.

Tower of London
www.toweroflondontour.com/kids/
The Tower of London is the oldest palace, fortress and prison in Europe. The fortress was created by William the Conqueror.

Wells Cathedral, Somerset
www.wellscathedral.org uk
The cathedral has massive columns topped with carvings of birds, animals, mythical beasts and ordinary people living in medieval England.

Winchester, Hampshire
A royal city from before the Middle Ages, Winchester's cathedral was the longest church in Europe when it was built. Cathedral Close contains many medieval buildings. The Hospital of St Cross, is the oldest almshouse in England. The medieval Great Hall is all that survives of the castle. Behind it is Queen Eleanor's Gardens, a recreation of an early medieval garden.

York
The medieval city walls, including two four-storey, fortified gateways, remain. The Merchant Adventurers' Hall has a timbered great hall and an undercroft and chapel. The Shambles is an area of medieval streets, lanes and alleys. The medieval churches include York Minster.

INDEX